This journal belongs to

_____

Date

_____

To him who is able to do immeasurably more than all we ask or imagine,

according to his power that is at work within us, to him be glory!

EPHESIANS 3:20-21 NIV

INTRODUCTION

Many of us have our lives planned out. Some of us are shooting
for the American dream of education, travel, career, marriage, kids,
and retirement. There are those who want to make it big while others
prefer to quietly work behind the scenes. Some crave contentment while
others hope to set the world on fire in one way or another.

God has a plan for our lives too. Sometimes His plan resembles ours.
Sometimes it doesn't. But His plan is always bigger and better
than anything we can plan for ourselves. He asks us to trust our future,
our plans, our every decision to His guidance.

As you make the daily decisions that affect the path of your life,
use this journal to keep track of the thoughts, prayers, challenges,
and triumphs of the journey. Our prayer is that you will never forget
that wherever the path may lead, God is with you.

THE EDITORS

What we feel, think, and do this moment influences both our present and the future in ways we may never know. Begin. Start right where you are. Consider your possibilities and find inspiration...
to add more meaning and zest to your life.

ALEXANDRA STODDARD

Commit to the Lord whatever you do,

and he will establish your plans.

PROVERBS 16:3 NIV

A woman of beauty…knows in her quiet center

where God dwells that He finds her beautiful,

and deems her worthy, and in Him, she is enough.

JOHN AND STASI ELDREDGE

Clothe yourselves...with the beauty that comes from within, the unfading

beauty of a gentle and quiet spirit, which is so precious to God.

1 PETER 3:4 NLT

There is nothing like a dream to create the future.

VICTOR HUGO

Hope deferred makes the heart sick,

but a dream fulfilled is a tree of life.

PROVERB 13:12 NLT

Society needs people who...know how to be compassionate and honest....
You can't run the society on data and computers alone.

ALVIN TOFFLER

What happens when we live God's way? He brings gifts into our lives…

things like affection for others, exuberance about life…a sense of

compassion in the heart, and a conviction that a basic holiness

permeates things and people.

GALATIANS 5:22-23 MSG

Inasmuch as anyone pushes you nearer to God,

he or she is your friend.

_____

_____

_____

_____

_____

_____

_____

_____

_____

_____

_____

_____

_____

_____

_____

_____

_____

_____

_____

_____

_____

_____

_____

_____

_____

_____

It is good and pleasant

when God's people live together in peace!

PSALM 133:1 NCV

Your future is as bright as the promises of God.

A. JUDSON

No eye has seen, no ear has heard, and no mind has imagined

what God has prepared for those who love him.

1 CORINTHIANS 2:9 NLT

I trust You always, though I may seem to be lost
and in the shadow of death. I will not fear, for You are ever with me.
And You will never leave me to face my perils alone.

THOMAS MERTON

The Lord is my shepherd; I shall not want. He makes me to lie down in green pastures; He leads me beside the still waters. He restores my soul.

PSALM 23:1-3 NKJV

God's love never ceases. Never.... God doesn't love us less if we fail or more if we succeed. God's love never ceases.

MAX LUCADO

_____

_____

_____

_____

_____

_____

_____

_____

_____

_____

_____

_____

_____

_____

_____

_____

_____

_____

_____

_____

_____

God promises to love me all day,

sing songs all through the night!

My life is God's prayer.

PSALM 42:8 MSG

God cares for the world He created, from the rising of a nation to the falling of the sparrow. Everything in the world lies under the watchful gaze of His providential eyes, from the numbering of the days of our life to the numbering of the hairs on our head.

KEN GIRE

Look straight ahead, and fix your eyes on what lies before you.

Mark out a straight path for your feet; stay on the safe path.

Don't get sidetracked; keep your feet from following evil.

PROVERBS 4:25-27 NLT

God never abandons anyone on whom He has set His love; nor does Christ, the good shepherd, ever lose track of His sheep.

J. I. PACKER

If God cares so wonderfully for wildflowers that are here today
and thrown into the fire tomorrow, he will certainly care for you.

MATTHEW 6:30 NLT

God has designs on our future...and He has designed us for the future.
He has given us something to do in the future that no one else can do.

RUTH SENTER

_____
_____
_____
_____
_____
_____
_____
_____
_____
_____
_____
_____
_____
_____
_____
_____
_____
_____
_____
_____
_____
_____
_____

"For I know the plans I have for you," declares the LORD,

"plans to prosper you and not to harm you,

plans to give you hope and a future."

JEREMIAH 29:11 NIV

Beauty puts a face on God. When we gaze at nature,
at a loved one, at a work of art, our soul immediately recognizes
and is drawn to the face of God.

MARGARET BROWNLEY

I will give thanks to You, for I am fearfully and wonderfully made;

Wonderful are Your works, and my soul knows it very well.

PSALM 139:14 NASB

We may not all reach God's ideal for us, but with His help
we may move in that direction day by day as we relate
every detail of our lives to Him.

_____

_____

_____

_____

_____

_____

_____

_____

_____

_____

_____

_____

_____

_____

_____

_____

_____

_____

_____

_____

_____

From now on every road you travel

Will take you to God.

Follow the Covenant signs;

Read the charted directions.

PSALM 25:10 MSG

Whatever God tells us to do, He also helps us to do.

DORA GREENWELL

The Holy Spirit helps us in our weakness. For example, we don't know
what God wants us to pray for. But the Holy Spirit prays for us
with groanings that cannot be expressed in words.

ROMANS 8:26 NLT

Every day we live is a priceless gift of God, loaded with possibilities to learn something new, to gain fresh insights.

DALE EVANS ROGERS

SURETE
LE BOU
18SE
'19

This is the day the LORD has made;

We will rejoice and be glad in it.

PSALM 118:24 NKJV

Your looks at this age are a gift. You received them from your ancestors. But if you are still beautiful when your hair is gray and your bones ache, that beauty is from your own doing.

My cup brims with blessing.

Your beauty and love chase after me

every day of my life.

PSALM 23:5-6 MSG

A dream becomes a goal when action is taken toward its achievement.

BO BENNETT

I focus on this one thing: Forgetting the past and looking forward
to what lies ahead, I press on to reach the end of the race
and receive the heavenly prize.

PHILIPPIANS 3:13-14 NLT

I would rather walk with God in the dark
than go alone in the light.

MARY GARDINER BRAINARD

You are a chosen people, a royal priesthood, a holy nation,
God's special possession, that you may declare the praises of him
who called you out of darkness into his wonderful light.

1 PETER 2:9 NIV

Try to keep your sense of humor! When you can see the funny side of a problem, sometimes it stops being so much of a problem.

EMILIE BARNES

_____

_____

_____

_____

_____

_____

_____

_____

_____

_____

_____

_____

_____

_____

_____

_____

_____

_____

_____

_____

_____

_____

_____

_____

_____

Now, God, do it again—

bring rains to our drought-stricken lives...

So those who went off with heavy hearts

will come home laughing, with armloads of blessing.

PSALM 126:4-6 MSG

Don't judge each day by the harvest you reap
but by the seeds that you plant.

ROBERT LOUIS STEVENSON

SURETY
LE BO
18SE
'19

Plant your seed in the morning and keep busy all afternoon,

for you don't know if profit will come from

one activity or another—or maybe both.

ECCLESIASTES 11:6 NLT

The victory of success is half won when one gains the habit of setting goals and achieving them. Even the most tedious chore will become endurable as you parade through each day convinced that every task, no matter how menial or boring, brings you closer to fulfilling your dreams.

OG MANDINO

Seek first God's kingdom and what God wants.

Then all your other needs will be met as well.

MATTHEW 6:33 NCV

God's Word acts as a light for our paths. It can help scare off unwanted thoughts in our minds and protect us from the enemy.

GARY SMALLEY AND JOHN TRENT

SURET
LE BO
18SE
'19

Your word is a lamp for my feet,

a light on my path.

PSALM 119:105 NIV

Our Creator would never have made such lovely days, and given us the deep hearts to enjoy them, above and beyond all thought, unless we were meant to be immortal.

NATHANIEL HAWTHORNE

The whole earth is full of His glory!

ISAIAH 6:3 NKJV

When the world around us staggers from lack of direction,
God offers purpose, hope, and certainty.

GLORIA GAITHER

Everything has already been decided. It was known long ago
what each person would be. So there's no use
arguing with God about your destiny.

ECCLESIASTES 6:10 NLT

In God's wisdom, He frequently chooses to meet our needs by
showing His love toward us through the hands and hearts of others.

JACK HAYFORD

Serve each other with love. The whole law is made complete in this
one command: "Love your neighbor as you love yourself."

GALATIANS 5:13–14 NCV

We do not want merely to see beauty, though, God knows, even that is bounty enough. We want something else which can hardly be put into words—to be united with the beauty we see, to pass into it, to receive it into ourselves.

C. S. LEWIS

I'm asking God for one thing, only one thing:

To live with him in his house my whole life long.

I'll contemplate his beauty; I'll study at his feet.

That's the only quiet, secure place in a noisy world.

PSALM 27:4-5 MSG

Go confidently in the direction of your dreams.

Live the life you have imagined.

HENRY DAVID THOREAU

There is surely a future hope for you,

and your hope will not be cut off.

PROVERBS 23:18 NIV

There are high spots in all of our lives, and most of them come about through encouragement from someone else.

GEORGE ADAMS

Encourage one another and build up one another,

just as you also are doing.

1 THESSALONIANS 5:11 NASB

God has not promised sun without rain,

Joy without sorrow, peace without pain.

But God has promised strength for the day,

Rest for the labor, light for the way.

ANNIE JOHNSON FLINT

I will lead the blind by ways they have not known, along unfamiliar paths

I will guide them; I will turn the darkness into light before them

and make the rough places smooth.

ISAIAH 42:16 NIV

God never abandons anyone on whom He has set His love;
nor does Christ, the good shepherd, ever lose track of His sheep.

J. I. PACKER

Yea, though I walk through the valley of the shadow of death, I will fear no evil; for You are with me; Your rod and Your staff, they comfort me. You prepare a table before me in the presence of my enemies.

PSALM 23:4-5 NKJV

Time is a very precious gift of God; so precious that it's only given to us moment by moment.

AMELIA BARR

_____
_____
_____
_____
_____
_____
_____
_____
_____
_____
_____
_____
_____
_____
_____
_____
_____
_____
_____
_____
_____
_____
_____
_____
_____
_____
_____

Be careful how you live.... Make the most of every opportunity....

Don't act thoughtlessly, but understand what the Lord wants you to do.

EPHESIANS 5:15–17 NLT

Together we will forge a pathway up the high mountain....
Though the path is difficult and the scenery dull at the moment,
there are sparkling surprises just around the bend. Stay on the path [God]
has selected for you. It is truly the path of life.

SARAH YOUNG

You will show me the path of life;

In Your presence is fullness of joy;

At Your right hand are pleasures forevermore.

PSALM 16:11 NKJV

It is pleasing to God whenever you rejoice
or laugh from the bottom of your heart.

MARTIN LUTHER

In this world you will have trouble. But take heart!

I have overcome the world.

It's what you learn after you know it all that counts.

HARRY S. TRUMAN

Let the wise listen and add to their learning,

and let the discerning get guidance.

PROVERBS 1:5 NIV

Don't be afraid to take a big step if one is indicated;

you can't cross a chasm in two small jumps.

DAVID LLOYD GEORGE

May he give you the power to accomplish all the good things

your faith prompts you to do.

2 THESSALONIANS 1:11 NLT

The price of success is hard work, dedication to the job at hand, and the determination that whether we win or lose, we have applied the best of ourselves to the task at hand.

VINCENT T. LOMBARDI

May He grant you according to your heart's desire,

And fulfill all your purpose.

PSALM 20:4 NKJV

Because God is responsible for our welfare, we are told to cast all our care upon Him, for He cares for us. God says, "I'll take the burden—don't give it a thought—leave it to Me." God is keenly aware that we are dependent upon Him for life's necessities.

BILLY GRAHAM

I lay down and slept,

yet I woke up in safety,

for the LORD was watching over me.

PSALM 3:5 NLT

Giving is a joy if we do it in the right spirit. It all depends on whether we think of it as "What can I spare?" or as "What can I share?"

ESTHER YORK BURKHOLDER

Each of you has received a gift to use to serve others.

Be good servants of God's various gifts of grace.

1 PETER 4:10 NCV

Lift up your eyes. Your heavenly Father waits to bless you—

in inconceivable ways to make your life what you never dreamed it could be.

ANNE ORTLUND

I will lift up my eyes to the mountains; From where shall my help come?

My help comes from the LORD, who made heaven and earth.

PSALM 121:1-2 NASB

Get into the habit of saying, "Speak, Lord,"
and life will become a romance.

OSWALD CHAMBERS

Nothing in all creation will ever be able to

separate us from the love of God.

ROMANS 8:39 NLT

Whenever it is possible, choose some occupation which you should do even if you did not need the money.

WILLIAM LYON PHELPS

Do your work with enthusiasm. Work as if you were serving the Lord,

not as if you were serving only men and women.

EPHESIANS 6:7 NCV

Becoming a leader is synonymous with becoming yourself.

It is precisely that simple, and it is also that difficult.

WARREN G. BENNIS

Anyone who belongs to Christ has become a new person. The old life
is gone; a new life has begun! And all of this is a gift from God.

2 CORINTHIANS 5:17–18 NLT

Whoever walks toward God one step,

God runs toward him two.

JEWISH PROVERB

A person's steps are directed by the LORD.

How then can anyone understand their own way?

PROVERBS 20:24 NIV

If you have never heard the mountains singing, or seen the trees of the field clapping their hands, do not think because of that they don't. Ask God to open your ears so you may hear it, and your eyes so you may see it, because, though few people ever know it, they do, my friend, they do.

PHILLIPS MCCANDLISH

You will go out in joy and be led forth in peace;

the mountains and hills will burst into song before you,

and all the trees of the field will clap their hands.

ISAIAH 55:12 NIV

The true meaning of life is to plant trees,
under whose shade you do not expect to sit.

NELSON HENDERSON

It's not important who does the planting, or who does the watering. What's important is that God makes the seed grow. The one who plants and the one who waters work together with the same purpose.

1 CORINTHIANS 3:7-8 NLT

Today is unique! It has never occurred before and it will never be repeated. At midnight it will end, quietly, suddenly, totally. Forever. But the hours between now and then are opportunities with eternal possibilities.

CHARLES R. SWINDOLL

Go after a life of love as if your life depended on it—because it does.

Give yourselves to the gifts God gives you.

Most of all, try to proclaim his truth.

1 CORINTHIANS 14:1 MSG

There never was any heart truly great and generous,
that was not also tender and compassionate.

ROBERT SOUTH

Be agreeable, be sympathetic, be loving, be compassionate, be humble....
Bless—that's your job, to bless. You'll be a blessing and also get a blessing.

1 PETER 3:8-9 MSG

Nothing is as real as a dream. The world can change around you, but your dream will not. Responsibilities need not erase it. Duties need not obscure it. Because the dream is within you, no one can take it away.

Every good action and every perfect gift is from God.
These good gifts come down from the Creator of the sun, moon, and stars,
who does not change like their shifting shadows.

JAMES 1:17 NCV

Do you want to be wise?

Choose wise friends.

CHARLES SWINDOLL

A sweet friendship refreshes the soul.

PROVERBS 27:9 MSG

Heaven often seems distant and unknown,
but if He who made the road...is our guide,
we need not fear to lose the way.

HENRY VAN DYKE

I am always with you;

you hold me by my right hand.

PSALM 73:23 NIV

God, who has led you safely on so far, will lead you on to the end. Be altogether at rest in the loving holy confidence which you ought to have in His heavenly providence.

FRANCIS DE SALES

The LORD directs the steps of the godly.

He delights in every detail of their lives.

Though they stumble, they will never fall,

for the LORD holds them by the hand.

PSALM 37:23-24 NLT

A study of the nature and character of God is the most practical project anyone can engage in. Knowing about God is crucially important for the living of our lives.

J. I. PACKER

Continue in what you have learned and have become convinced of, because
you know those from whom you learned it, and how from infancy you have
known the Holy Scriptures, which are able to make you wise.

2 TIMOTHY 3:14-15 NIV

God is every moment totally aware of each one of us. Totally aware in intense concentration and love.... No one passes through any area of life, happy or tragic, without the attention of God with them.

EUGENIA PRICE

The LORD protects those who are loyal to him.

PSALM 31:23 NLT

You can't experience success beyond your wildest dreams
until you dare to dream something wild!

SCOTT SORRELL

God can do anything, you know—far more
than you could ever imagine or guess
or request in your wildest dreams!

Life is not easy for any of us. But what of that? We must have perseverance and above all confidence in ourselves. We must believe that we are gifted for something and that this thing must be attained.

MARIE CURIE

God blesses those who patiently endure testing and temptation.

Afterward they will receive the crown of life that God has promised

to those who love him.

JAMES 1:12 NLT

Our greatness rests solely on the fact that God in His incomprehensible goodness has bestowed His love upon us. God does not love us because we are so valuable; we are valuable because God loves us.

HELMUT THIELICKE

The LORD is good; his steadfast love endures forever.

Leadership is a combination of strategy and character.

If you must be without one, be without the strategy.

H. NORMAN SCHWARZKOPF

_____

_____

_____

_____

_____

_____

_____

_____

_____

_____

_____

_____

_____

_____

_____

_____

_____

_____

_____

_____

_____

_____

_____

And patience produces character, and character produces hope.

ROMANS 5:4 NCV

The measure of a life, after all,
is not its duration but its donation.

CORRIE TEN BOOM

Give, and it will be given to you. A good measure, pressed down,

shaken together and running over, will be poured into your lap.

For with the measure you use, it will be measured to you.

LUKE 6:38 NIV

There are no shortcuts to any place worth going.

BEVERLY SILLS

We are merely moving shadows,

and all our busy rushing ends in nothing....

And so, Lord, where do I put my hope?

My only hope is in you.

PSALM 39:6-7 NLT

Even when all we see are the tangled threads on the backside of

life's tapestry, we know that God is good

and is out to do us good always.

RICHARD J. FOSTER

We know that in everything God works for the good of those who love him.

They are the people he called, because that was his plan.

ROMANS 8:28 NCV

We learn more by looking for the answer to a question...

than we do from learning the answer itself.

LLOYD ALEXANDER

You will search again for the LORD your God. And if you search for him
with all your heart and soul, you will find him.

DEUTERONOMY 4:29 NLT

Everyone has a unique role to fill in the world and is important in some respect. Everyone, including and perhaps especially you, is indispensable.

NATHANIEL HAWTHORNE

Just as each of us has one body with many members,

and these members do not all have the same function....

We have different gifts, according to the grace given us.

ROMANS 12:4-6 NIV

The road to the head lies through the heart.

AMERICAN PROVERB

Trust in the Lord with all your heart; do not depend
on your own understanding. Seek his will in all you do,
and he will show you which path to take.

PROVERBS 3:5-6 NLT

They are well guided that God guides.

We can make our plans,

but the LORD determines our steps.

PROVERBS 16:9 NLT

A little kindly advice is better than a great deal of scolding.

FANNY CROSBY

Kind words are like honey—sweet to the soul and healthy for the body.

PROVERBS 16:24 NLT

A span of life is nothing. But the man or woman who lives that span, they are something. They can fill that tiny span with meaning, so its quality is immeasurable, though its quantity may be insignificant.

CHAIM POTOK

I pray that you…will have the power to understand the greatness of Christ's love—how wide and how long and how high and how deep that love is…. Then you can be filled with the fullness of God.

EPHESIANS 3:18–19 NCV

$\mathbb{G}$od created us with an overwhelming desire to soar.... He designed us to be tremendously productive and "to mount up with wings like eagles," realistically dreaming of what He can do with our potential.

CAROL KENT

Those who hope in the LORD will renew their strength.

They will soar on wings like eagles; they will run and not grow weary,

they will walk and not be faint.

ISAIAH 40:31 NIV

You learn something every day if you pay attention.

RAY LEBLOND

Pay attention to what I say; turn your ear to my words.

Do not let them out of your sight, keep them within your heart.

PROVERBS 4:20-21 NIV

Recognizing who we are in Christ and aligning our life with God's purpose for us gives a sense of destiny.... It gives form and direction to our life.

JEAN FLEMING

You guide me with your counsel,

leading me to a glorious destiny.

PSALM 73:24 NLT

Get over the idea that only children should spend their time in study.

Be a student so long as you still have something to learn,

and this will mean all your life.

HENRY L. DOHERTY

Teach the wise, and they will become even wiser;

teach good people, and they will learn even more.

Do not dwell upon your inner failings…. Just do this:
Bring your soul to the Great Physician—exactly as you are,
even and especially at your worst moment…. For it is in such moments
that you will most readily sense His healing presence.

TERESA OF AVILA

Then Christ will make his home in your hearts as you trust in him.

Your roots will grow down into God's love and keep you strong.

EPHESIANS 3:17 NLT

We are so preciously loved by God that we cannot even comprehend it.
No created being can ever know how much and how sweetly
and tenderly God loves them.

JULIAN OF NORWICH

I have loved you with an everlasting love;

I have drawn you with unfailing kindness.

JEREMIAH 31:3 NIV

Beauty is also to be found in a day's work.

MAMIE SYPERT BURNS

My heart rejoiced in all my labor;

And this was my reward.

ECCLESIASTES 2:10 NKJV

The secret of life is that all we have and are
is a gift of grace to be shared.

LLOYD JOHN OGILVIE

Many people will praise God because…

you freely share with them and with all others.

2 CORINTHIANS 9:13 NCV

W̲e are made to persist.

That's how we find out who we are.

TOBIAS WOLFF

Keep on asking, and you will receive what you ask for. Keep on seeking, and you will find. Keep on knocking, and the door will be opened to you.

LUKE 11:9 NLT

Do well the little things now and then great things
will come to you by and by, asking to be done.

PERSIAN PROVERB

Well done, good and faithful servant! You have been faithful
with a few things; I will put you in charge of many things.

MATTHEW 25:21 NIV

God's wisdom is always available to help us choose from alternatives we face, and help us to follow His eternal plan for us.

GLORIA GAITHER

Listen…and be wise, and set your heart on the right path.

PROVERBS 23:19 NIV

In waiting we begin to get in touch with the rhythms of life—
stillness and action, listening and decision. They are the rhythms of God.
It is in the everyday and the commonplace that we learn patience,
acceptance, and contentment.

RICHARD J. FOSTER

May he keep us centered and devoted to him, following the life path

he has cleared, watching the signposts, walking at the pace

and rhythms he laid down for our ancestors.

1 KINGS 8:58 MSG

Ellie Claire® Gift & Paper Corp.
Brentwood, TN 37027
EllieClaire.com
A Worthy Publishing Company

For I Know the Plans I Have for You
2013 Journal
© 2013 by Ellie Claire Gift & Paper Corp.

ISBN 978-1-60936-815-9

Scripture references are from the following sources: The New Revised Standard Version Bible (NRSV),
Copyright 1989, 1995. Division of Christian Education, National Council of Churches of Christ in the
United States of America. Used by permission. The Holy Bible, New International Version® NIV®. Copy-
right © 1973, 1978, 1984 by Biblica, Inc.™ Used by permission of Zondervan. All rights reserved world-
wide. The Holy Bible, The New King James Version (NKJV). Copyright © 1982 by Thomas Nelson, Inc.
Used by permission. The Holy Bible, New Living Translation® (NLT), copyright © 1996, 2004, 2007 by
Tyndale House Foundation. Used by permission of Tyndale House Publishers, Inc., Carol Stream,
Illinois 60188. The Message (MSG) © 1993, 1994, 1995, 1996, 2000, 2001, 2002 by Eugene Peterson.
Used by permission of NavPress, Colorado Springs, CO. The New Century Version® (NCV). Copyright ©
1987, 1988, 1991, 2005 by Thomas Nelson, Inc. Used by permission. All rights reserved. The New
American Standard Bible® (NASB), Copyright © 1960, 1962, 1963, 1968, 1971, 1972, 1973, 1975,
1977, 1995 by The Lockman Foundation. Used by permission. All rights reserved.

Excluding Scripture verses and deity pronouns, in some quotations references to men and
masculine pronouns have been replaced with gender-neutral or feminine references. Additionally,
in some quotations we have carefully updated verb forms and wordings that may distract modern readers.

Cover and interior design by David Carlson | StudioGearbox.com
Typesetting by James Baker | aestheticsoup.net

Printed in China

4 5 6 7 8 9 – 18 17 16 15